RELATED REVIEWS

Peggy O'Neill Mack: "Tim has always been versatile with words. I've seen and heard him stammer them, sing them, slur them, and hurl them. Glad to see he can write them too."

Matt O'Neill: "When I asked Timmy why he began the book in Purgatory, he quickly replied, 'Will Rogers began in Oklahoma.' "For his sake, buy this book; for yours, read it and embrace it."

Dennis O'Neill: "Tim had a four-year head start on me reaching for the bowl of potatoes. It was almost as much fun reading these stories as it was watching most of them as they happened."

Kevin O'Neill: "Tim was seventeen when I was born. Mom and Dad had me instead of a second car. Tim forgave me on the day of my wedding. Twenty-four years is a long time to hold a grudge; fifty-seven years is an even longer time for Tim to have stalled writing this entertaining book."

Amy O'Neill: "I just read this and have elevated Uncle Timmy to fourth favorite uncle."

Tessa & Addie Rose O'Neill: "Uncle Timmy was already our fourth favorite uncle."

TOBACCO
IS NOT A VEGETABLE

By Tim O'Neill

Lin:

Hope you enjoy "Tobacco is not a Vegetable." Will be interested in your call whether I end up in Heaven or Purgatory ... not that there is anything wrong with that.

Best,

Tim O'Neill

ISBN-10: 061563639X
ISBN-13: 9780615636399

TIM O'NEILL V. PURGATORY

I have a dream. I hope it doesn't actually occur for at least two decades. It takes place in the waiting room outside St. Peter's Gate. It isn't heaven, but heaven is nearby.

In this dream, I get a glimpse of Purgatory on the way up. It doesn't look too bad: tract homes and tons of franchise joints. I am waiting because my lead presenter in the case of *Tim O'Neill v. Purgatory* is at my funeral. My presenter is a successful surgeon named Big Iowa.

I watched my wake on the big screen in the waiting area last night. I'm hoping today's funeral mirrors it with many more laughs than tears. As friends begin to gather in the church, I zoom in on a lively conversation between Horn, Reggie and Wils. It appears a big wager is being propositioned about the length of the service. Horn is setting the over-under total at 54 minutes. I think to myself the under is a lock. No way my brothers would pick anything but a fast priest for this one.

It had been simple for me to narrow the list of my presenters to St. Pete to two: Big Iowa and Doc Rames. Both are surgeons. Both are sons of town doctors from the Midwest. And they are the only two friends I've ever had who did not have at least a thimbleful of devil in them. I want this "St. Pete Meet" to be a saint-to-saint thing!

When long-time pal Billy the Sheet passed the week before I did and selected Doc Rames as his St. Pete presenter, my choice became clear. It would be Big Iowa. I knew the case of *Billy Cady v. Purgatory* would require intense preparation and at least a week in trial. Rumor had it that Heaven's Arena would sell out for that one, and a few of Heaven's marginal members created a Stub Hub for the trial. Word had trickled down that some tickets were priced as high as a thousand holy days of obligation. No, Billy Cady is not *flawful*; let's say *flaw-*

some! It should suffice to say that Billy will get lots of cheers and jeers from both sides of the aisle.

Looking toward the big screen, I see Big Iowa entering my funeral. On his arm is his lovely wife, Maria. His three incredibly talented and attractive kids trail. The Big Iowa is wearing a broad smile as he greets my wonderful brood. He is solid.

To assist Big Iowa, I have prepared more than fifty distinct life lessons learned from more than one hundred characters that left indelible marks on a life that traced the border between Heaven and Purgatory. What follows are those stories. The Big Iowa will sort through these and compose a compelling sequence.

Advertising legend David Ogilvy once cautioned writers to "never write more than two pages on any subject." I'm glad to report *Tobacco Is Not a Vegetable* is in compliance with Ogilvy's sage advice.

I bet Big Iowa will get me into Heaven the same way I had been accepted into several prestigious schools, companies, and clubs…barely!

Four wonderful friends who always have my back.
This time they are to my left: Doc Rames, Big Iowa, BK, and John D.

BK

My first round as a Bellerive Country Club member was memorable, not for the golf, but for the lunch conversation afterward. Two very distinct foursomes merged at a big table. The group I had endured for the previous four hours was horrific at golf but even worse at conversation. Conversely, the other group appeared to be normal. They joined us because our table was the only spot available.

Men's Grill topics generally run the gamut, but our conversation ventured into uncharted territory when one of the cads I had been paired with tossed out the question, "What is it, mates, that you find most enjoyable to do with your wife?" My mind immediately went to positions. But a member of my foursome volunteered, "Gardening." Another dimwit suggested, "Opera." As the newest member, I remained quiet and pondered whether the entire membership could potentially be this dull.

Just before our fourth guy could follow with something equally absurd—like maybe "the symphony"— there was a sign of something positive; the handsome guy from the other foursome, a guy who called himself BK, piped up with, "Airport." The gardener and the opera lover raised their eyebrows. "BK, 'airport?' Pray tell?" asked Opera. "Is that meant to inform us that your favorite thing to do with your wife is to travel?" With even more conviction than his first outcry, BK charged back with, "Airport! As in, my favorite thing to do with my wife is to drop her off at the airport."

All my worries about being unable to strike up a friendship at this club were over. This was a potential best friend. And today he is!

BK and I have recounted this story dozens of times over the past twenty-three years. Okay, his reply was funny. And it was partially true, as all strong relationships benefit from short breaks. The real art of his reply was his ability to shift the nature of a conversation. He zoomed it from boorish to flourish—by colliding clarity with hilarity!

Another truism that was confirmed to me that day was that whom you play with is far more important than where you play. I'll take a fun group on a nine-hole municipal course with scraggy greens over a bunch of dullards on a world-class course any day—not to say that a fun group on Sand Hills or Pebble Beach wouldn't be the best combination.

BK and Raybo Hooting & Hollering

RED HEAT

If he actually managed to swallow all the red wine he poured, a case could be made that Red Heat is an alcoholic. Considering how much he spills before he can swallow it, his consumption does not even approach that of the average social drinker. His white golf shirts could be matted, framed, and sold as lovely watercolors. One shirt with a merlot splash looked identical in shape to a map of the Caribbean. It even had a nacho drip located on Puerto Rico.

The Heat's golf game has a lot in common with his red wine. He spills in sand shots, flops, chips, and long putts almost every hole. His game around the greens reminds me of watching someone shoot pool on a tilted table. During one round, we were playing with Jay Williamson, a longtime PGA Tour veteran. Jay couldn't believe the Heat. "I've never seen anything like this," he said. Considering Jay's weekly playing partners have names like Tiger, Phil, and Sergio, this was a compelling observation.

Last Saturday, I played the Heat. He shot even par without hitting a green. One drive was under a fence. Two were in the trees. Another was on a bridge. And he shoots a seventy-two!

What can you say about Red Heat that hasn't been muttered before by an opponent? My salute is to his dogged pursuit of recovery from difficulty, something the Heat does incredibly well in golf and in life. Guts! That's the one thing the Heat never spills. No, Red Heat never spills his guts.

Billy the Sheet with his rival Red Heat

THE SHEET

So Red Heat fares well in most of his golf outings. The exception is one opponent who just has his number. That would be BC, a.k.a. Billy the Sheet; a.k.a. Billy Plumb Bob; and a.k.a. many more nicknames not suitable for mixed company. It's okay to have one player who always has your number. However, it's preferable that opponent not be in your regular foursome. BC is called "the Sheet" because he carries a piece of paper where he lists how much money each of his friends owes him. The Sheet would rather be owed than collect.

During one outing in Scotland, Red Heat and the Sheet went out to dinner. The Heat walked back to the hotel after spilling three merlots. The Sheet stayed out learning to play bagpipes and teaching the locals a thing or two about rum. Staggering through the hotel lobby at 6:10 a.m., the Sheet requested wake-up calls for 6:30 and 6:45. When the desk clerk inquired as to whether he meant a.m. or p.m., the Sheet slurred something that sounded like "aim" as he zigzagged to his room.

When the wake-up calls to the Sheet's room went unanswered, the bell staff went to the room to awaken their rum-swilling guest. Unable to move him, they reached out to Red Heat, asking that he "collect the body." At first, the Heat thought the Sheet was a goner. Unfortunately for the Heat, the Sheet arose and went on to birdie the first hole at Gleneagles forty minutes later, and the Sheet tallied another entry in Red Heat's column.

Watch out for opponents who can rise quickly from near death. The Sheet has sent me reeling many times. Still, it's fun to have a friend who calculates his winnings on paper versus one who actually expects payment.

BURNING SENSATION

When people ask me what finally drove me to quit smoking, I tell them "my legs." Let me explain. It was a two-day tournament which included a first night reception. After dinner, a "let's play cards for an hour" became an all-nighter for me and three of the other entrants. As my 7:30 a.m. tee time approached, I decided on a shower to restore some much needed energy. After drying off, I took aim at my underarm with the deodorant and missed, confirming how difficult it would be to break 80 in the second round.

One of my rituals as I prepare to golf is to place two dimes to serve as ball marks for the greens in my front, right pocket. Then I place two golf balls and a handful of white tees in my front, left pocket. This accomplished, I staggered to the #1 tee and found well-rested friends B-Love, Guirl-Man, and D-Lish arguing about who was going to be stuck with me as their partner for some high-stakes side bets.

My first hole included a mulligan and was highlighted with a sympathy gimme for double bogey. Approaching the #2 tee, I lit up a Marb Light. As I teed my ball, I tossed the half-smoked, lit cig to the ground and hit a mediocre drive. Mistaking the Marb Light for my tee, I picked it up and placed it my left pocket. Several minutes later, I found myself in the fairway with a sudden, sharp pain in my left thigh. B-Love looked at me and shouted, "Timmy, your shorts are on fire!" Acting on impulse, Guirl-Man furthered the pain by quickly dousing the fire with his hot coffee. Then, D-Lish, validating he of the finest lip wedge in the club, offered his immediate condolence of "it is never good to have a burning sensation in your shorts."

So, tobacco is not a vegetable and some things are not as they appear. And as I am reminded of that morning which finally convinced me to quit smoking, it should be easier to hit an underarm than a fairway.

FIRST **BIG** PITCH

I spent weeks developing my first big presentation for incentives industry leader, Maritz. It involved a potential sponsorship deal for convenience store giant 7-Eleven at the 1984 Olympics in Los Angeles. I spent every last moment leading up to my mad dash to the airport refining my pitch.

I was prepared. The presentation would be a hit. I had packed my new khaki suit, which would be perfect for a summer day in Texas. The only item I had not checked off my list of things to do was polish my shoes. This was important because the leader of our account team was a West Point grad. Though I did not have time at the airport to complete my list, I recalled a shoeshine stand in my Dallas hotel.

The morning of the big pitch finally arrived. I was a little anxious when I discovered the shoeshine stand was not yet manned. The front desk informed me there was a shoeshine machine in the men's restroom across the hall.

So as I began rehearsing my lines for the presentation, I began enthusiastic application of my shoes to the machine—until I discovered brown shoe polish climbing the left leg of my new khaki suit! As if that weren't bad enough, the machine had eaten a tassel off my left loafer. Panicked, I raced to the concierge, who began to calm me. Her first instruction was to return to the restroom and retrieve my tassel.

As I got down on my knees and reached for the tassel, the restroom door banged open, hit my rear, and vaulted me face first into the shoeshine machine. I stood and discovered that not only was I missing a tassel, I had shoe polish on my nose and forehead as well on the leg of my new khaki suit. Adding further to my plight, I now found my knees nicely soaked with urine from having knelt on the squishy restroom floor.

Distraught, I headed to our Dallas office, where one of the assistants helped me clean up. Hours later, my boss's boss's boss, the West Pointer, closed the big pitch with my shoe polish story, exclaiming, "There are three ways to gain new sales: one is to be lucky, another is to be good, and a third is to have prospects feel sorry for you. Now, we feel lucky to have this opportunity to support 7-Eleven. Our recommendations are very good for you and your people. And to cover all three bases, don't you feel just a little sorry for that young man over there in the khaki suit?"

There are indeed three ways to gain new business. Better to rely on being good or lucky than on pity. But pity can work if it's all you've got.

FOURTH & D'S

School: The only grades I didn't like were fourth and D's. Didn't like fourth grade because of the teacher. And the D's? Those were a teacher issue as well.

JESUITS ROCK

Jesuits are remarkable teachers. They employ many techniques. One is story-telling. It is an approach they have employed long before it came to be in vogue. The following events took place in the fall of 1968. They taught me about discovering my strengths and the importance of brevity.

I had targeted St. Louis University High as my school of choice since third grade. I felt great about this selection until a few minutes into my first day. A revered Jesuit priest, Father Kellett, hosted the first morning assembly of the freshman class. He was the first man of God I had encountered who also had the booming voice of God. He needed his cane to walk, but he didn't need a microphone to address 226 trembling freshmen. He had the look of a taller and thicker Spencer Tracy.

At the three-minute mark, Father Kellett paused and asked us to take a minute to scan the room, size up our new classmates, and "look 'em all in the eye." After twenty seconds he blistered us with, "Damn it, what kind of bullywhacks do we have in this class? I make one simple request—for each of you to take a good, hard look at each other—and you remind me of turtles going into a shell. Now, one more time, take a good, hard look at each of your new classmates. Five minutes…beginning right now!"

O'Boy, did these 225 other boys suddenly look impressive through this new lens of insecurity. Each one either looked smarter, stronger, more handsome, or older than I was—and by a wide margin. We were clearly unaware that this eye-balling marathon was an intentional ploy to bring us down and then back up.

After three hundred seconds slowly ticked by, Father Kellett announced, "Okay. Let's make something clear. Only one of you will be valedictorian; only one of you will be quarterback of the football team; only one of you will be editor of the school paper; only one of you will be the lead in the school play; and only one of you will date the prettiest girl from St. Joseph's Academy." After a long pause, Father Kellett continued: "But each and every one of you is better than every one of us…at something. Now we only have four years to discover your unique strength, and that's not very long. So scram! Outta' here!" Yet we remained in place, frozen by the moment, temporarily paralyzed by this swift surge of inspiration. Then Father Kellett broke into the warmest smile. That's when we began to believe.

Weeks later, I shared with my dad how difficult high school was. What made it most challenging was that all the kids seemed so smart. Then my dad startled me by saying, "Yep, you won't have dumb kids in your class again until college." This proved to be true.

Soon after this revelation, I experienced another teen-changer. It was with my favorite teacher, another Jesuit, Father Sheehy (or, as my dad referred to him, "your Irish English teacher.") He was passing out graded essays to the class. The scores were numeric, and I snuck glances at grades ranging from seventy-five to ninety-five. Then I received mine. Rather than a score, it had a comment on it: "See me after class." I was bewildered because I had not cheated on this assignment as I had the paper turned in the day before for my history class.

After all the other boys had filed out of the classroom, I sheepishly approached Father Sheehy. He had my paper in his hand, and he affectionately swatted my shoulder with it. Then he said, "Timmy, let's make this a moment you will always remember." Then he took a red pen and drew a big circle around what seemed to be almost a full page. Then he wrote: "Forty-six words, one sentence. Always take the time to write a short one. And don't forget, two-syllable words are twice as powerful as four-syllable words."

My memories of these two Jesuits remain vivid. The first's call to discover your unique strengths, and the second's linkage of brevity to clarity were, and remain, compelling. However, it is *how* they did it that had the most impact. Storytelling can be your best way to connect.

If Big Iowa flies me past the Pearly Gates, I will relish time in the Jesuit Section, particularly at Story Time.

ROOM 112

The Jesuits didn't make many mistakes. This experiment was more fart than art or science. They decided to group the thirty kids who had accumulated the most demerits as freshmen into the same sophomore homeroom. It reminded me of the prison-break thriller *Con-Air* that was released several years ago. The only salvation was that the remaining 190 sophomores faced fewer distractions.

Imagine the excitement Fredman, Hawker, RJ, Wayco, Hono, Wood, Moz, the Reef, Otis, Shorty, Sully, and I felt our very first morning. Though we would go on to establish all-time records for most demerits in a day, week, month, and semester, we settled down a bit after funnyman T.B., whom we had elected class president, was expelled. Nevertheless, grouping the worst of the worst together is risky, whether it is a cellblock or a homeroom.

Eventually Jesuit power prevailed, and we began to reserve our antics for the weekends. Our group nickname became the Annual Boys because we would stage "annuals"—as in "best party of the year"—almost every weekend.

A four-letter word to describe this group is glee. Give credit to the Jesuits for converting us from "me" guys to "we" guys by giving us rope, but not enough rope to hang ourselves.

Surrounded by Room 112 ringleader Wayco and brother Matt circa 1984

HAUGHTY & NAUGHTY

After graduating from Mizzou's Journalism school, my search for employment included radio and television stations, newspapers, and advertising agencies. O'Wow, was I fortunate to discover a magical opportunity. It was with a people-centered company called Maritz. Headquartered in St. Louis, it was, and still is, the leader in the incentive industry. Maritz helps its clients achieve growth by motivating their employees, distribution channels, and customers. Some of the top rewards in the programs Maritz fulfills for clients are elaborate group trips and events. Invariably, the winners are top employees, salespeople, or customers.

Many of us have experienced the pressures surrounding a wedding that has a one-hour church service and a three-hour reception. Imagine the intensity when the event is not one day but six, possibly in a foreign environment, and every detail needs to be flawless for hundreds—possibly thousands—of a Fortune 500 company's most important people. Maritz includes onsite travel directors on all such trips to confirm and reconfirm every last detail of each activity from sunrise until well after sundown.

Every year Maritz hires between twenty-five and thirty new travel directors from a group of hundreds of candidates. While interviewing for this select position, I had no idea my last name had made a difference. The hiring manager was Jim McIlreavey, and he believed the two most important attributes for this position were cheerfulness and a sense of guilt. He wanted young people who had natural good cheer, yet felt enough guilt to responsibly make early wake-up calls even if he or she had been partying hours after all the clients had gone to bed.

McIlreavey believed young Irish folk had the perfect blend of those crucial qualities. So the Class of '76 featured a roster that included Tom O'Rourke,

Mike McCarthy, Kevin McDonough, Michael Pritchard, Susie O'Grady, Cathy O'Brien, Colleen Noonan, John Kearney, Doug Mackey, and fortunately for me, Tim O'Neill, among its headliners.

The class also included overseas talent. One was a Brit named Brian Chase. He looked like Michael Caine after having gone through a trash compactor. The only thing bigger than his tummy were his glasses. He had grown up in London and was an aspiring thespian. He later became a successful actor on the London stage. He was very funny in a British way. I called him Haughty. He was!

Michael Pritchard was a personal favorite from the Irish-influenced Class of '76. Like Brian, he was an aspiring entertainer, and he had been popular at local comedy clubs. His post-Maritz days include many screen credits and awards. Today he is a successful motivational speaker. He was a big lug of a guy who grew up in North St. Louis, which is even more the opposite London than all the other parts of St. Louis. He looked a bit like John Wayne and a pilgrim, too. I called him Naughty. He was!

I loved Haughty and Naughty, but I did not enjoy being with them together. Though they were the two most gifted entertainers of our extended team, I was not savvy enough to understand their natural rivalry. One trip we worked together was a chartered Caribbean cruise for General Electric. Haughty, Naughty, and I had worked a double shift the prior day, so as the ship docked in St. Thomas, the three of us were granted five free hours. We immediately found a hut in the hills for some rum chugging.

Acting as referee between Haughty and Naughty was the hardest work I had all week. I would have preferred supervising optional ship activities like the uphill burro ride or the not-so-precious jewelry-making tour. They sparred endlessly until Naughty evidently hit too low when he said something about the queen. That's when Haughty stood up to the imposing Naughty with a barrage that would become my lifelong theme: "Michael, you midget of a mind. Beat me if you must. Bash me if you will. Just don't booooooore me."

There is a lot to be said for preferring to be beaten or bashed rather than bored.

CASH V. NON-CASH

After four early teenaged years of caddying, my dad felt it was time for me to make a career path change. A friend of his helped me make the move from serving the country club set to the geriatric set. My dad's friend was the very funny and even feistier Mrs. Rose. She presided over a chain of four retirement homes and hired me to work the Sun Rooms at each property.

I would learn "working" the Sun Room meant purposeful narrow losses at cards and board games. I became quite artful at barely losing games that summer. Unfortunately, narrow losses is a skill set that has followed me for forty years with strings of bad beats involving the NFL, NBA, and NCAA.

Dad said I would learn a lot from Mrs. Rose. One lesson has been particularly memorable. It was during a conversation celebrating my one-month anniversary. She began by congratulating me on several close call gin rummy losses to three of her most cheerful patients. Then she asked me what I thought of my supervisor. With glee, I remarked how positive and productive he had become the past several days. Her eyes twinkled and asked if she could share with me a little secret. Then she told me how my supervisor had asked for a raise ten days earlier. And her response was "No, Michael, it is not in the budget for a raise right now but effective tomorrow, you can call yourself a 'Vice President' and you get to wear a coat and tie to work each day."

That was my first experience of watching the power of non-cash rewards. Little did I know then that I would spend the majority of my career with Maritz, the industry-leading provider of non-cash rewards.

Big Iowa shared with me one of his strategies for St. Peter was to cite my decades of experience in non-cash have prepared me to experience a heaven where non-cash is the way.

LIZ

Travel directors grow close working side by side while tending to the pressure-packed challenges of herding hundreds of folks who are not in their natural element. I became particularly close to a fun-loving gal named Liz. We were responsible for a charter full of Ford dealers en route from Chicago to Bali. Though we were working, our first "date" aboard this charter included more quality time than I'd had with my prior girlfriend, a woman I had dated for almost two semesters.

Liz and I were engaged within a year. Two things happened at our engagement party that should have been telltale signs for Liz. I was wearing my favorite white flannel pants and was just leaving my rental home headed for the party when my disgruntled landlord arrived. He was glaring at a car battery in the middle of the front yard. I quickly picked it up and tossed it into the backseat of my Oldsmobile.

I noticed some stains across my pants and dismissed them as drops of water from the battery. No, it was battery acid. Thirty minutes into the party, I felt a draft. The right leg of my pants had begun to dissolve. A coat-and-tie function, and I suddenly looked like one of the Flintstones. I was wearing cut-offs! Of course, my backseat was a goner, too.

And the pants were not the worst of it. Minutes later, I took a bite into a cocktail tomato that was harder than a Titleist. The innards flew more than twenty feet before landing on the neck of a distinguished lady who was friendly with Liz's family.

A fun wedding and the purchase of a fixer-upper soon followed. So why didn't we make it? Well, the fixer-upper didn't help. St. Joseph may have been a carpenter, but evidently, St. Timothy was not. Liz grew up in a wonderful family that prioritized housework and home improvement. My family was top-drawer, too. As in, all of our tools were in our top kitchen drawer. Liz's family had tons of tools to help with the fixer-upper. My dad's favorite song was "If I Had a Hammer" because he didn't. Liz's family fixed leaks; mine fixed drinks.

Growing up, we didn't even have a rake. When Mom asked us to rake, my brothers and I would troll the neighborhood for filled leaf bags and reposition them in front of our yard. So Liz was married to a guy with two left hands whose idea of a lengthy to-do list was to pick up the dry cleaning *and* empty the dishwasher.

If the pre-wedding party should have been a tell for Liz, certainly the "celebration" of our first anniversary provided confirmation that trouble lay ahead. Because my parents' relatively young neighbor had unexpectedly passed away that day, I approached the evening with a gloomy feeling. The festivities were to be held at a classic St. Louis restaurant called Busch's Grove. We had requested seating in one of the outside huts.

As we arrived, Liz excused herself to use the restroom. I remained outside watching a flurry of bugs flying in the air. When Liz returned, she saw a crowd gather around her panicked husband. A pair of bugs that were mating had flown inside my ear. Two tuxedoed waiters came to my rescue. One was older, tall, and thin. I would soon discover the shorter, younger one had a better knack with visual imagery than predicting the future. When I told them about the sex scene going on in my ear, the lean, older gentleman broke into song. With his hands slapping his knees, his deep voice intoned, "You gonna die… You gonna die." To which the younger tux broke into song with "…happened to my uncle…ate away half his brain."

Well, I darted across the street to the fire department, and the EMTs rushed me to St. John's emergency room. When I queried the ambulance driver for his read on my status, he shook his head and said, "Damnedest thing I ever heard." Recovery immediately ensued when a doctor in the emergency room drowned the sex offenders.

Weekends in our first two years were dominated with projects around the fixer-upper. Liz's dad was a fun guy and talented with his toolbox. He didn't seem to mind my following him around like a pup, handing him the tool he needed, much like an operating room nurse does with a doctor during surgery. The problem was I didn't know what most of the tools looked like. It took some doing, but I did learn that a Phillips screwdriver didn't have anything to do with orange juice.

On more than one occasion, I could be heard to mutter, "My next home is a nursing home." Not an inspiring phrase for a twenty-something bride to hear from her twenty-something groom.

One Saturday morning, Liz called me from her parents' house and said they finally had a project with which I could help. They were tearing down their screened-in porch. The thought was I could master the skill of tearing off shingles. Within an hour, I made it to the roof. A minute later, I'd made it twelve feet south to the concrete floor. I'd stepped through a soft spot, fracturing both the concrete and my skull. Hours later at the hospital, my dad sensed I needed to be humored and challenged. "What is an O'Neill doing on a roof if he is not breaking into a house?" he said.

The skull fracture caused some changes. One was a newly discovered ability to slur words and do it very slowly without needing a drink beforehand. Every word was thickly tongued. Prior to the fall, Maritz had slotted me for a promotion either to New Jersey on the AT&T account or to Detroit for General Motors. It took just one hospital visit from my boss, the Shogie, for a change of plans. Liz and I were soon dispatched to open a Maritz office in Oklahoma.

Oklahoma began with another fixer-upper. However, I vowed to bring a positive attitude to the new weekend assignments. That's why my first purchase in Tulsa was an electric lawnmower with a cord four feet shorter than the perimeter of our yard. This created an entertaining way for me to cut through a chore. I made the quick release of the cord and the four-foot finish before the motor cut off a new skill set. Always important to make even the mundane experiences more entertaining!

My fall through a roof that led to an articulation problem and a relocation to Oklahoma proved to be a blessing. The assignments to Detroit or the East Coast were all about holding onto existing large accounts. The Oklahoma assignment was all about landing new business. Retaining accounts and developing new ones are two different sports. My experiences and the confidence I gained selling new accounts in Oklahoma stood me well as I progressed to sales and sales leader roles.

Today, at age fifty-eight, Liz remains as attractive as any woman in St. Louis. She also did extremely well in her second round of marriage. Her husband is a successful attorney and politician with a sterling reputation. His name is Mike, and they have a lovely daughter, Meredith. And together with me, we share major talent in Liz and my son, Danny, as well.

SISTER ROBERTA MARIE

The consensus of grade-schoolers at Mary Queen of Peace was that the nuns were stricter than our parents. This made sense as many families in the parish were of Irish descent. Word on the playground among fourth-graders was: enjoy your time now because the fifth grade teacher, Sister Roberta Marie, was grizzlier than her moustache.

Fifth grade was challenging; in part because of Sister Roberta Marie but also because of Ronnie, a disruptive kid in class. Ronnie saw himself as quite the comic. One day as we were studying fractions and percentages, Ronnie pressed his game with fake farts and other noise adventures. Sister sensed Ronnie's peers had tired of him and asked Ronnie to come to the front of the class. Then she wrote on the blackboard:

$9/10 = \underline{\hspace{1cm}}\%$ $1/10 = \underline{\hspace{1cm}}\%$

Sister challenged Ronnie to complete the simple math. He completed the blanks correctly but couldn't answer Sister's question about why she selected those two equations. When he couldn't answer, Sister told a life-changing stunner about a supposed research study she had read the night before. She said it revealed that ninety percent of Americans were capable of being fun, yet only ten percent of us are funny. She went on to congratulate Ronnie for being part of the majority, the ninety percent who could be fun. She then strenuously warned him about the troubles facing those other than the select ten percent when they tried to be funny.

Her callout went something like this: "Ronnie, comedy is serious, and you are so much in that ninety percent number. Fun is okay, but your attempts at funny are fruitless. Feel blessed that you are not cursed with the talent to be funny."

Well, Ronnie grew up in a big way that day. So did our class. We became more productive. And we became more serious about fun than funny. When fifth grade was complete, I was more prepared for sixth grade than I had been for prior advances.

Yes, if my ticket to the big H does indeed get punched, I will definitely visit the Convent section and thank sister for her valuable math lesson.

Trying to be funny when you are not is a common mistake. The most frequent abusers are recently promoted male executives. People selected to hit numbers should adhere to the ten percent rule. Some CEOs can pull off both leadership and humor: Southwest Airlines' Herb Kelleher, Nestle Purina's Pat McGinnis, and Maritz's Steve Maritz, to name three.

MOM

The setting was a noisy, three-generation Thanksgiving dinner. The surrounding sound was two dozen O'Neill's. Most were in at least two simultaneous conversations. A singular topic emerged: "What is your very favorite thing to do?" Golf. Dance. Snowboard. Travel. Attend Cardinals games. Eat at restaurants. Play basketball. Two more "golf's." Reading also got a mention.

The buzz quieted when Mom paused after saying, "My very favorite thing to do is…" Then she said, "Visit. I love to visit." Her kids and grandkids went immediately quiet. To visit. Isn't "to visit" really why we golf, go to restaurants, dance, and go to Cardinal games?

In one of our last visits, Mom shared a concern about cell phones and the younger generation's ability to connect. She felt cell phones and text messaging disrupted the attention needed for robust dialogue. Mom thought that cell phone etiquette should become a required high school course, perhaps leading to certification; much like a sixteen-year-old must earn a driver's license before being allowed behind the wheel.

Mom was an exceptional visitor. She always made whoever she was with her priority. Coincidentally, Mom's schooling was at Visitation Academy.

CITY KIDS

My dad volunteered to start a football program at Mary Queen of Peace for the sixth, seventh, and eighth graders. The first thing he did was order kelly green uniforms rather than the royal blue long associated with Mary, Mother of God, a shade that had been Mary Queen's staple color for decades.

I began attending practices in second grade. It was fun being around the older boys, particularly as a fifth-grader when the team won a city championship. The team stumbled during my era before regaining prominence when my younger brother, Denny, was the star quarterback and his best friend, Billy Lynch, was the stud lineman. Dad would often say, "I have had stronger offensive lineman, but none as smart as Billy. He is the only one I've ever coached smart enough to understand how to hold and not get penalized."

Denny, Billy, and I still reminisce about Dad's halftime speech at their championship game. The game was tied 7–7. Keep a few things in mind. First, Dad grew up in a modest Irish neighborhood in the heart of the city. He remained a "city kid" forever. His team, Mary Queen of Peace, was in an upper-middle class neighborhood clearly considered more upper crust than that day's opponent.

Attempting to infuse as much energy into the team as possible, Dad's halftime tirade disregarded facts and called out the opponent as a bunch of cocky, spoiled, rich suburban kids and reminded the players that our team needed to show them how tough "we city kids" could be.

Our team of sons of doctors, lawyers, and businessmen—their imaginations suddenly drained of their creature comforts—burst out of the locker room with an unprecedented intensity and flattened their opponent. The city kids won with a convincing 28–7 victory.

People are both emotional and rational. We need to consider both when pushing buttons to gain agreement. Pushing only the emotional button has a short shelf life—about as long as the second half of a grade-school football game.

In a dream Heaven, there are no grade schoolers. If a few try out, I'll coach them with extreme care.

NOOOOO RESTRICTIONS

Marty Brennan and my dad celebrated their golden anniversary of getting each other into and out of trouble when they reached fifty-five years of age. A decade later, Dad was in the hospital. Though the cancer was grim, he was not. After four endless days, Dad reached out to his reliable friend who went to the hospital, dressed Dad, evaded hospital staff, and returned him to his favorite chair at home. Immediately, Dad poured a double vodka and lit back-to-back Tareytons.

Mom was startled beyond belief by what she mistakenly hoped had been a miracle. As she watched Dad with his drink and cigs, she asked about his release from the hospital. He shrugged. When she asked about the doctor's specific orders, he smiled and said, "Just two words: 'Nooooo restrictions!'"

Then he winked at me and said, "Tobacco is not a vegetable."

The very best friendships are all about nooooo restrictions. His didn't have them. Mine neither. I miss him!

When Big Iowa finesses my application past St. Peter, Dad will be the first angel I seek out. He will be easy to find, most likely holding court in Heaven's smoking section.

He called himself Donald James "Knockemstiff" O'Neill

SOREN P

I wasn't nervous about college until a few seconds after my dad and younger brothers hustled out of Mizzou and headed back to St. Louis. I recalled a curious conversation a sage sophomore had shared at registration a month earlier about how male college freshmen are the lowest form of human life. Could he be right?

My roommate had yet to arrive, but a handout on the bottom mattress indicated his name was Soren P. Sorensen III. I imagined Scandinavian royalty, perhaps a navigator. I would soon discover his navigation was limited to brew specials, and the only thing royal about him was the color of his date-night blue boxers. My dad had said his name was Danish. He arrived soon after, and a first glance confirmed a likely appetite for many such pastries.

Soren P was built like a dining room table. His head and his hairstyle were total flattop. Though he was six feet four inches, his legs were as trunky as they were short. His belly was fuller than most, but it was even longer than it was wide. He looked really tall in a chair. The poor guy was the only student on campus who didn't own a pair of jeans. Levi Strauss didn't make "44 W–26 L's" in 1972.

Soren P's two claims to fame were a thunderous laugh and coming in second place at Greek Week's beer chugging competition for six consecutive years. He declined his final year of eligibility when the event organizer wanted to list him as a seventh-year freshman rather than a fourteenth-semester senior.

This was an era when Johnny Carson ruled comedy and his second chair was filled by the continuous laughter of Ed McMahon. Soren P was a lot like Ed, only with a better laugh. There wasn't anything second place about the way we all felt listening to his *harrumph*. A better sound I have never heard. And I never will until St. Peter says "you're in."

College buds Hono, Galva, and Soren P

WHEN TOO MUCH SEX
ED IS TOO MUCH SEX ED

Soren and I would best friend a transfer student who was galvanizing campus. We called him Galva. He had a bankroll. He had a wardrobe. And he had a dune buggy. He was fleshy. He was tan. And his shiny black hair looked navy blue when the light hit it just right. I told him once he looked like a blue jay that had just finished a big meal.

Speaking of colors, Galva was revered by bartenders in town for his "maroons," which were a shot of Johnnie Walker Red and a shot of Johnnie Walker Black.

Galva was always considerate. A good example was the regular visits to St. Louis where he would stay at my family's home. During most visits, we would return home well after midnight. During all visits, Galva's final move was to the hamper which he would unload and create a makeshift bed of the dirty clothes. He would then retrieve my three-year-old brother Kevin from his single bed and place him gently on the clothes pile but always positioning Kev's head away from the socks and boxers. That opened up space in Kevin's bed for Galva to begin his snore.

Galva and I decided to run together for president and vice-president of Mizzou's student council. As weeks progressed, we were pleasantly surprised to be considered one of two tickets with the potential win. Our polls revealed the only fraternity we weren't carrying was Galva's frat house.

The opposing ticket was led by a highly respected gal who had impressed me in three classes we had shared. She would burst our bubble when she confided to me we were ineligible because my running mate didn't meet the sole requirement of full-time student status. Evidently, Galva's only class that semester was a three-hour class on sex ed. Keep in mind that Columbia, Missouri was a small town in the 1970s but it was home to three colleges: University of Missouri, Stephens College, and Columbia College. It would leak later that Galva's semester also included three hours of sex ed at Stephens and Columbia, too. Gratefully, his semester did not include a sex ed class at Columbia's only high school.

That qualified gal on the opposing ticket would go on to do an outstanding job leading the student council. One of her first roles was to host a campus tour of then President Gerald Ford. Upon graduation, she moved to Washington, DC and enjoyed a distinguished career. Today, there is a street named after her in Columbia. If Galva and I had won, we would probably have an alley named after us. And who could guess how we would have done with a President Ford who was infamous for his frequent stumbling.

Lessons learned. Best to apply for positions which you are indeed prepared and qualified. As for the sex ed, considering I am a parent of two in college, I'd prefer their sex ed be the Galva Way—in a classroom versus a dorm room.

JAZZMO

The first time I met "Jazzmo" Johnnie Johnson was my sophomore year at Mizzou. Four of us were assembled around a picnic table in a mutual friend's backyard. A large bottle of scotch stood on the table, and a running hose was at our feet. Sure, I had drunk scotch and soda before. And scotch on the rocks, too. But scotch and hose? Heaven forbid we get up to grab some water when a running hose was available.

Jazzmo would go on to best me at ping-pong and foosball later that night, at golf the next day, then beat me out of a date with a mutually-desired coed the next night. It would have been nice if Jazzmo had informed me he was at Mizzou on a golf scholarship before arranging the golf bet. It would be thirty-five years until I bested Jazzmo at anything. Let me explain.

Jazzmo was not just on a golf scholarship. He would captain Mizzou's team and go on to establish himself as one of the top amateurs in the Midwest, if not the country. My bucket list included beating him just once in one of our annual matches. Though our geography was never a match after college, we made a point to schedule one round each year. Between 1975 and 2009, Jazzmo's record against me was spotless. The 2010 match was set to take place at my club in St. Louis. I had the greenskeeper set most of the pins to the right half of the greens, the better to receive my slicing shots. And I financially motivated our best caddie, Chris, to purposefully misread Jazzmo's putts by just an inch. Chris would pile on with some yardage fractures as well. Game on.

Jazzmo had a dozen lip-outs, and somehow I was able to scratch another item off that bucket list. As I gloated, he mumbled something like, "Cats are sleeping with dogs." A week later he called with instructions to check my mailbox. I did. Jazzmo evidently didn't want me to have a full year of self-esteem and had overnighted an airline ticket to Chicago.

I soon learned that, as club champion more than a dozen times and a long-time board member of a prestigious club overlooking Lake Michigan, his reach with the staff had more distance than my fades. I suspected something was up when the first hole pin was located two steps from the left fringe. No, cutters do not like tucked left pins. Second hole, same. Third hole, even closer to the left fringe. Each of the eighteen holes that day was tucked left! Paradise for Jazzmo, the opposite for me. Jazzmo had only one bogey, and I had to sneak in a ten-footer to tie that one. He won the other seventeen holes.

That night we returned to his house and waxed nostalgic about the old days, even partaking in several scotch and hoses. As evidenced every week on television, home-field advantage is real in sports. At work, too. Anytime you can control your environment, take advantage. Schedule meetings in your office whenever possible. And when all else fails, hit your backyard for a scotch and hose.

TUTOR TIM

In my last two years at Mizzou, the football team knocked off Alabama, USC, Ohio State, and Nebraska, all as road underdogs, which paid back handsomely on some risky wagers.

I figured the least I could do was help some of these good guys stay eligible. It required a unique approach. It began with making certain they signed up for classes dependent on papers and essays instead of multiple-choice tests. Writing their papers was the exact opposite of the assignments I'd had in Journalism school, where the approach was to get something down on paper and then make it better. With the football players, the approach was to get something down on paper and then make it more believably worse. It was fun.

For classes with essay tests, we wouldn't open the textbook. Rather, we would search the Internet of yesteryear, the encyclopedia, and master just one takeaway per topic. For multiple-choice tests, the counsel was "man off the street:" sage advice about getting a good night's sleep, laying out comfortable clothes, and finding a homely gal to befriend who would share just a few answers.

The goal was to earn a C+, which also was the amount of effort they put in to close the season against Kansas. The loss cost me more than a month of pizzas. The moral of this story? Don't bet on teams with players for whom you have to dumb down their papers.

TGIMM, A.K.A. THANK GOD IT'S MONDAY MORNING

One Easter Sunday, my brothers Matt, Denny, and I sat in front of the television watching the final round of *The Masters*. Our wives were busy preparing dinner, and our collective eight preschoolers were romping all over the place. Finally, Aunt Mary Alice asked for just a little bit of help with the kids. Sometimes wives just don't understand the significance of sporting events and television. Denny sighed and said, "Remember a few years ago when we frequented TGI Friday's? Sometimes I feel that same way on Mondays. TGIM."

The next morning my desk phone was ringing as I scurried into my office. It was Matt, exclaiming, "TGIMM. Thank God it's Monday...morning!" Work can be so much fun if we are careful to select an industry and an occupation that fits us. It is so important to map out a career journey that plays to your strengths.

MY FIRST JOB & THE LAST FIB

The Maritz travel directors of today attend intensive training for eight weeks prior to going on-site with a client. In 1976, training was an afternoon workshop with three breaks. I was neither well-traveled nor well-qualified. I remember, though, having the common sense to ask a friend, not a Maritz person, for directions to the St. Louis airport. My one takeaway from training was to respond to any client who inquired about how long you had been with Maritz by saying, "less than a year."

My second client trip was to Boca Raton, Florida. I was having a time of it, searching for lost luggage with an uptight, East Coast client contact. He was all over me. He demanded to know, "How long have you been with Maritz?" I obediently followed with the correct, scripted response from training. I was not prepared, however, for his second question about my favorite destinations. I improvised with a fabrication about how Maritz travel directors specialize in specific destinations. When he asked my assignment, I responded with my two spring break destinations of Fort Lauderdale and Lake of the Ozarks.

Two months later, after client trips to Monte Carlo, Paris, London, and Hawaii, I realized the absurdity of my fib.

My supervisor was a steely veteran of six months named Jeff. He would become president of Maritz Travel some twenty years later. I confided to Jeff my rookie dialogue with the East Coast client about destination specialists. He lashed into me with something like, "Buyers don't like liars." He followed with, "If we ever do have a client choose the Ozarks for a trip, rest assured you will lead it." Jeff stressed the absolute power of truthfulness with clients. "Always, no matter what!"

The most successful leaders I have encountered are as passionate about honesty as they are about results. We never did recover that lost luggage, but I did recover from my last client fib!

I better remind Big Iowa of this no fib track record. *Thou Shalt Not Fib* is a commandment to revere, adhere, and endear.

YOUR TWO FEET

After thirteen glorious years with Maritz, I took on the president's role at a long-standing trade show firm called Heritage Communications. The staff included carpenters, decorators, and sign makers from three different unions, as well as designers, engineers, salespeople, and support staff.

Our primary product was the design and fabrication of trade show exhibits. Some were the size of a ping-pong table; others were the size of a football field. Trade shows are an opportunity for brands to demonstrate their offerings to buyers and consumers in a cost-effective way.

My initial challenge was to land new accounts so we would not be so over-whelmingly dependent on our top account, Anheuser-Busch. This proved to be a challenge, largely because our design team was so Budweiser-centric. It didn't matter if the prospect was a bank, a healthcare company, or a technology provider; all of our designs had the look of a pub or "19th hole." The decision-maker for a pitch at Nestle Purina was an old friend who cautioned, "Timmy, I said 'pup crawl,' not 'pub crawl.' For chrissake, our branding is about cats and dogs, not Clydesdales!"

The trade show industry rocked in the 1990s because it enabled many com-panies to launch new products with powerful results. Once, when I was ques-tioned as to how we differed from an ad agency, my response was, "They make commercials out of film; we make ours out of wood." We enjoyed success and were supported by an ownership group that invested in new people and tools to generate even more success.

I recall many engaging conversations with Ron, our principal investor. He had enjoyed success with both IBM and ABC before catching the venture capitalist bug and buying Heritage.

Let me share two takeaways from Ron that had great meaning for me. His first was a comment about salespeople hitting numbers. He shared his wariness for salespeople who thought they were hitting numbers when the only two they hit consistently were 8:30 and 5:00. The second was at a staff meeting when he approved a budget for some new things called "e-mail" and the "Internet." He warned that some companies had seen productivity declines after the arrival of e-mail because some employees used it frequently for personal reasons. Or worse yet, some used it as a critiquing tool because it is easier to hurl assaults from a keypad than in person.

Ron cautioned us against becoming too reliant on our computers. He reminded us about the importance of face time. It went something like this: If you are having an issue, use an even more important tool than your computer or telephone—your two feet! Use them to gain face time to solve a problem.

E-mail is a tool, not a weapon. Sometimes it is miraculously speedy. And sometimes it is much quicker to use those two feet and walk over for a face-to-face talk.

TWO BEST HIRES

Female tennis professionals peak around twenty. Baseball and football players peak around thirty. Salespeople continue to add to their game and do not peak until their late fifties.

That is why some think it best to hire salespeople in their forties or early fifties, nabbing them as they approach the top of their games. Turns out that this does not work well. Most companies retain their best sales talent at that age, and the pliable ones are expensive and, well, let's just say there usually is a reason they could be plied. My approach is to catch the most dynamic natural talent when you can afford them, which is usually when a person is in his mid-twenties and has experience at a company known for hiring only the most talented under-grads.

It has been my good fortune to hire many talented salespeople. The two most exceptional have been Fred and Liz. As twenty-something's working with me, both earned MBAs from prestigious business schools while far outpacing norms in their day jobs. And the brands for which they delivered conquest sales are top-drawer accounts.

When I get a résumé, I search to discover if our network has anything in common. When I discovered Fred had gone to the same university during the same era as the Kalmer One's oldest boy, Mark, I made a phone call. Mark is a one-percentile people-reader and his description of Fred was, "Really, really smart and always has a big smile." Hired!

When I read Liz's quality résumé, I tried to dissuade our HR VP from taking the time to interview her in New York. "Can't we just hire her over the phone?" Patience and good judgment prevailed. HR, as usual, was right. Liz in person was even more impressive than her best-ever résumé.

Polished, intelligent, poised, and really, really nice are these two: exceptional at work and exceptional with family. If salespeople don't peak until they are in their late fifties, it's hard to fathom how much better these two will be in thirty years.

Companies have many responsibilities as they navigate today's "new normal." One that cannot be overlooked is an effective search for, and nurturing of, their leaders of tomorrow.

GOOD COACH, BAD COACH?

Mike was a new salesperson. He knew I really liked him and his potential, so he tolerated my blunt coaching. My fierce candor was all about speedily ramping up our rookies. Without the need to finesse my communication, Mike was making rapid progress in learning to sell our solutions.

In fact, Mike dug up an opportunity that was outside our realm. The small project with very little upside clearly did not fit us. Eager to get on the board with his first sale, Mike scheduled a WebEx with the prospect and prodded me to join him. After vehemently listing all the reasons we should not take the appointment, I reluctantly agreed to attend.

The prospect went on and on about specifications that were outside our scope and beneath our budget threshold. I tried my best to politely rationalize why this was not a fit and provided the name of a company that was a better fit for her needs.

Well, I thought she had hung up and the call was over. I then began a rapid-fire assault on Mike. I railed about how ridiculous the call had been, reminding him (with a few expletives mixed in) of the reasons we shouldn't have made the call. Suddenly, Mike took on the look of a deer in headlights. No, it wasn't his reaction to my harangue. He realized the prospect was still on the line.

She immediately asked for the name of my supervisor. I apologized and provided the requested contact information. Unfortunately, we had just gone through a company-wide reorganization, and I barely knew my new boss.

Some say something good always comes out of something bad. My history with that saying is, maybe sometimes, but not always. In this instance, though, it did. An intense audit and lengthy interviews with my team led to the conclusion that this was an isolated incident. My team expressed appreciation for my direct communication style, saying they felt it led to speedier success. I owed my team for making them survive interrogations on my behalf. And I owe them even more for the way they are lighting up with new sales.

Technology can be your friend. It can be your enemy as well, particularly if you are a loose-lipped Irishman. Check, and then double-check, all video and audio devices that can potentially land you in hot water. Big Iowa and I will do just that as we rehearse *Tim O'Neill v. Purgatory*.

THE INSTITUTE

If I were asked to rank the twenty most talented people I have worked with, more than half would be women. Mary Beth is one who stands near the top of the list. That is why I am glad she heads the Maritz Institute.

To sustain leadership in the world of motivation, Maritz launched the Maritz Institute in 2009 and placed Mary Beth at the helm. If we are going to help corporations harness the potential of their people, we need to understand what makes people tick—and what makes them ticked. It's simple, really. People are at the heart of business.

The Maritz Institute is a deep dive into the human sciences and a collaboration of educators and business leaders. At its core is the groundbreaking work of Paul Lawrence and Nitin Nohria at Harvard. Their Four-Drive Model, which details the drives to acquire, bond, create, and defend, provides the cornerstone for the institute's approach to understanding human nature.

I told a peer that the five best presentations I had experienced last year were presented through the Institute. Unfortunately, the five worst were too. Some presenters lay out their words in a sensible and rhythmic fashion. Kudos to presenters who can make a seemingly complex topic like neuroscience sound simple.

Thanks to Mary Beth, Maritz is using brain-based people principles to optimize business outcomes for clients and their people. Said best, "better business and better lives." It's been fun working with a company helping clients accomplish both.

THE HOBO & LORI

It was a cold, wintry night. The checking account had taken hits from Christmas and some bad beats in the bowl games. It was time to cash in the change I had been collecting in the huge bowl on my dresser. For more than a year, I had emptied my pockets into my cash bowl. To my pleasure, it had become quite heavy.

I didn't feel good. I didn't look good. And my outfit was even worse—brown sweats topped by a purple hoodie covered by a black-and-blue windbreaker. I looked like a bruise, so I began my trek to the grocery store where a money machine would convert my coins to cash. I hoped nobody I knew would see me.

Midway through the cash exchange, I felt a tap on my shoulder. It was Lori. Now, every company worth its salt has that one woman whom everyone adores. At Maritz, that would be Lori. Smart. Attractive. Upbeat. So you can imagine my chagrin when she tapped my shoulder and said, "And that would be our vice president of sales."

There are times we look our worst. Just when you think you can go someplace as an incognito hobo, invariably you will run into someone. Best to dress it up a bit. You never know when you will run into an angel.

WOULDN'T TRADE 'EM FOR TWO LIKE 'EM

My dad used to hug me as a child and encourage me with a favorite line of his: "Wouldn't trade you for two like you." His tone was so endearing that I didn't process it to be a gentle stinger until I went away to college.

Well, I feel the same way about my coast-to-coast group of friends. I've observed groups of friends carry on forever and have never seen the charisma or entertainment value matched by those outside my circle. There are so many stories; I'll have to exclude some. That's why a sequel is an automatic.

The always lovely Sarah

SARAH

Sarah and I had a date. Then we had another. And another. When a mutual friend discovered this, he texted me, describing Sarah as "fun and classy." He could have added sweet, poised, and gorgeous and still hit a bull's-eye. I Googled "fun and classy" in search of a loftier two-word compliment. I couldn't find a better word, let alone two. Our friend's description was also code for "you better be nice to her."

Sarah shrugged when I called her out as "classy." She doesn't like the word. She thinks it is overused, restrictive, elitist, and almost haughty. So I looked up "classy" the old-fashioned way. The hardbound version defined "classy" as "elegant." I wish I had described her as elegant instead. She is.

A five-letter word Sarah lives is "cares." She cares hard for her four kids. She cares hard for her four sisters. She cares hard for close friends. When she describes defining moments—like a son's touchdown pass or hockey goal, or a daughter's exuberance or grade point average, or a feel-better session with a friend—the color of her presence goes neon. Conversely, when someone on Team Sarah is fending off one of life's slap shots, she is the first to be right there to deflect the pain.

Perhaps it is her nursing background, but Sarah can out-care the best. She is a living, breathing care package. Fortunate are those closest to her; fortunate for Sarah, too, because most return care to the sender.

I have thought about *O'Neill v. Purgatory*. Yes, Big Iowa has a lot of witnesses to summon. Unfortunately, so do St. Pete's prosecutors. If a compromise is needed, I could withstand a twenty-year stint in the Purg waiting for Sarah's certain first day ascent into the BIG H.

DOC'S SPEECH

Doc is an exceptional husband, father, son, brother, uncle, friend, and surgeon. Exceptional! His past includes an Illinois state championship in the high jump, college basketball, and last year he became the first golfer in the history of world-class Sand Hills Golf Club to close out its fierce final two holes with a pair of deuces. I am surprised Hollywood didn't nab him when he did his residency in Los Angeles. Along with his many other outstanding qualities, he looks like a leading man.

Doc idolized his older brother, Doug, when he was growing up. They were the two sons of the town doctor in Vandalia, Illinois. Unfortunately, Doug passed away from cancer in his forties. When Doug's kids approached marrying age, Doc crafted an important message to share with them.

We call it "Doc's Speech." It goes like this: "The most important decision you will ever make is not where you go to school, what you major in, or where you live. It is not your choice of occupation. Not to say those choices are unimportant, but they pale in comparison to your biggest decision…and that is clearly whom you choose to spend the rest of your life with in marriage. Nothing's close."

I first heard the speech at a holiday event when Doc presented it to his four kids. His daughter Lindsay said they had heard it more than ten times. And for Lindsay, that was four years and three boyfriends ago. Today, Doc is called upon to make this same speech to his friends' kids. It is a hit with the parents. Even when it leads to some eye rolling, the kids appear to acknowledge it as an important message—for the other kids.

Yes, Doc can fix your fibula or your tibia. And he is exceptional at getting inside your "ribia" with positive tugs to your heart and soul. His message about picking the right partner is on the mark. And the choice to marry his lovely wife, Sue, was a perfect important decision.

Smiles all around with the King and Doc Rames at King's Roast

THE KING

It would be difficult for almost anyone to live up to the nickname "The King," but the guy I call The King lives up to the title. His brother, John, bestowed the moniker when they were vacationing in Hawaii. John was overwhelmed by the lavish treatment afforded them because of his brother's longtime career in the travel industry. Treatment "fit for a king" quickly transitioned into a permanent tag for its recipient.

"Hello. My name is Jeff, but my friends call me King. And my even closer friends call me The King." How does someone make that kind of statement and actually endear himself? The only way! With a permanent smile and plenty of laughter. Consistent glee. And always positive...Always!

Several years ago, The King badly injured his left knee playing tennis. Doc Rames was summoned. Doc brought along his oldest boy, Richard. He wanted Richard to experience firsthand how someone with a positive attitude handles misfortune. Sure enough, despite a blown ACL, Doc and Richard were greeted not by a grimace, but by smiles interrupted by laughter.

Earlier this year, I was honored to be part of the dais for a celebrity roast to celebrate The King. It was one of those lifetime highs. In preparing for the event, I researched many of the old Dean Martin roasts popular back in the day. This Dean Martin quote struck me: "The key to a really good roast is not the quality of the roasters. It is all about the quality of the roastee."

That is why "The King's Roast" was a lifetime high. The man of the hour that evening is "all world" in the two important categories of smiling and positive attitude. So much more can be said (and heard) when it funnels through an ever-present smile. And so much more can be accomplished when it is fueled by a highly positive attitude. Long live the King!

THE SIMPSONS

The closest to a royal couple I know are BA and Leslie Simpson. Their closets are organized by fibers of cashmere, Egyptian cotton, linen, and striped silks. The only synthetic things they own are two golf umbrellas.

BA and Leslie winter on John's Island and summer on Cape Cod. This past summer's Cape Cod stay was surrounded by a week at Cypress Point in Carmel and a stately Long Island series that included Maidstone, Shinnecock, and National. Tonight, they return from Seminole.

So you may guess BA and Leslie to be rather exclusive…or at least elusive? Wrong! They are as warm and engaging as any couple I know. They just happen to have Gatsby looks and tastes.

When I meet someone from BA and Leslie's circle, I can quickly gauge the person's listening skills. It's all about their reaction to one question I always pose. "Don't you think BA is the wittiest person you have ever met?" To date, I have asked sixty-two people. Right now, the score is deadlocked at 31–31. Half give me a big smile and respond with something like, "I bring my best ears when I know I am going to be with BA. He is unbelievably clever!" The other half respond with a quizzical nod and maybe a "Pardon me?" I score them as self-absorbed, poor listeners. Actually, fifty percent with good listening skills is a fairly good score for a group that has grown up privileged.

As attractive a couple as I know, this pair leads any league in entertainment value. They bring words and facial expressions of endearment. Yet they can right size you in a hurry when a hushed wallop is in order.

Some people resent people who appear to have it all. It is better to revere them. And when successful people like BA and Leslie reach out to you with a compliment, do not be falsely humble. Look 'em in the eyes, smile, and say thank you.

LA WOMAN

My daughter Jane called from USC last summer to inform me that the mother of her new roommate, Taylor, had gone to Mizzou. When I countered with, "Maybe I know her. What was her maiden name?" Jane rallied with, "Dad, she is way, way younger than you. Way!"

Evidently USC doesn't offer a "Guess-their-age" class, because Taylor's mom is a gleaming gal named Paula with whom I was friends at Mizzou. And yes, we were in the same graduating class. She was a beauty in school. Still is! She is an LA looker!

I have noticed, both as a son and as a parent, that kids tend to think their parents are older than they are, and parents tend to act as if their kids are younger than they are.

WOOD PILE

Doug has been a friend since college. He is almost always a gentleman. He wasn't yesterday though when he suggested his "wood pile" was better than mine. He was referring to our exes. Frankly, I disagree.

I recall one of his former girlfriends whenever the subject of bad blind dates comes up. Doug's then girlfriend was a nice gal who grew up in Boston. A childhood friend of hers was visiting St. Louis and I agreed to go out with her. As blind dates go, she clearly saw only herself. She couldn't stop talking about Boston and railed at St. Louis. Tired of the snub, I asked her opinion of stereo-typing, and she didn't seem to understand. So I followed by asking whether she thought New Yorkers walked and talked faster than Kansans, and she replied with a resounding, "Of course."

I then began to ask how she felt about people from Bahs-Bahs-Bahs and paused. Sensing the Bahs-Bahs-Bahs was a hesitating abbreviation for Boston, she insisted I continue. So, yes, I asked her how she felt people felt about people in Boston. I have always been amazed how many Bostonians regard themselves as brilliant just because they breathe the same air as Harvard. She kept pushing for my reply. With sufficient pause, I said softly: "dim."

My blind date was astonished. When she challenged, I explained that we were in the midst of a technology revolution. Keep in mind this was circa 2000 and the following company names were freshly "tombstoned." I recounted how the Boston-based technology giant Wang had a chance to be the technology indus-try leader but had over-depended on its local Boston workforce and had been beaten by the competition. The same story applied to former Boston-based technology giant Digital Equipment Corporation. Too dependent on its Bos-tonian labor.

Rushing to a close, I shared with her how the most innovative companies in the technology sector had learned from their mistake and were now reaching out geographically to the more intelligent communities in western North Carolina, south Texas, and northern California.

No offense, Boston, but visitors need to play nice. I am certain each town has a percentage of folks who carry themselves like my blind date. Not to stereotype, but my guess is it is a higher percentage among Bostonians than Kansans. Then again, Kansans...

Every family needs either a Scapegoat or a Jayhawk. We took on a Jayhawk named Al shown here on the left with my brothers Matt and Denny

WOOD

Had you asked my friends in high school to name their favorite actor, almost all would have named Brando, Redford, Newman, DeNiro, or Pacino. My friend, Wood, would have named someone else. His favorites were always the guy in trouble whom the cops couldn't turn. Recently, Wood told me that the way Paul Sorvino handled prison in *Goodfellas* was his all-time favorite.

One time in high school, seven of us committed a series of pranks. The school principal was not happy. When he discovered Wood had a hand in the treachery, he wanted more names. We knew Wood would never crack, and we were in the clear. He is the only one I know who's earned an epitaph of "I never snitched."

It's no secret that keeping secrets is a key to keeping friendships.

LINCOLN'S LAWS

When my slope gets slippery, I speed-dial into the Philadelphia Main Line and am greeted by my highly confident friend, Lincoln. When I think of Lincoln, I am reminded of a favorite Ralph Waldo Emerson quotation: "The friend in my adversity I should always cherish most. I can better trust those who helped to relieve the gloom of my dark hours than those who are so ready to enjoy the sunshine of my prosperity."

Lincoln is a man of many gifts. Sometimes his best gifts are words I do not want to hear. Yes, he is a blast when things are going well. And yes, he has a way of blasting you into reality when it is time for you to pick yourself up.

R. Waldo's quotation is on the mark. Many of us need to do a better job of creating quality time for friends in need.

NIECES

I fondly recall family reunions every Sunday at my grandma's house. Her name was Babe O'Toole. As a matter of fact, the only relatives there without an O' were the Murphy's.

One of my favorite television shows is *David Feherty,* shown on the Golf Channel. I don't just watch his show: I study it. He is so much more than just funny. He is the most transparent interviewer in television.

Watching Feherty reminds me of how I approached those Sunday events at Babe's. I recall straining with all my might to take in all of the chuckling one-liners by my aunts and uncles. I paid the same close attention to my relatives then, as I do now to Feherty. Something unpredictable and funny is almost always just a moment away.

Whatever degree of conversation skills I have developed were honed by observing my upbeat relatives. As a kid, I studied the generation ahead. Today, I watch the generation below, particularly my eleven nieces, who couldn't win a foot race but are hyper-quick with clever one-liners. Sharply quick and pretty. Maybe quick wit skips a generation?

One of the reasons I am counting on Big Iowa propelling me skyward is I will want to spend decades making Heaven a better place to receive these angels many-many years from now.

GTO

I grew up in a home with many rules, but only two that were enforced: "Be nice to your brothers," and "Be nice to your brothers." One morning my mother announced we were to have a family meeting that evening. Though we continually met as a family, we had never experienced a scheduled meeting.

At the time of this meeting, I was seventeen, Matt was sixteen, Denny was thirteen, and Peggy was only six. In preparing for the meeting, we first challenged each other about what any of us had done wrong that might have led to this unprecedented event. In so doing, we discovered another unprecedented event: it was the first moment in memory when none of us could think of anything we had done wrong. Or at least there was nothing we'd been caught at.

With two of us now driving, Matt offered up the possibility that Mom and Dad had scheduled this meeting to announce they were buying us a car, something we clearly could not afford. I countered with, "I bet it is a GTO. Dad knows how much I want a sports car." Then arguments broke out over how we would share. Even thirteen-year-old Denny weighed in about his access. His rationale for gaining the keys was all about it being a sports car, and he was "the best of all of us at sports." We were frenzied. With zero facts to support the belief our robust wish was about to be fulfilled, we became convinced a new GTO was in play.

We approached our first family meeting with zest. Almost immediately, Mom and Dad announced another sibling was six months away. The family wasn't getting another car, but a car seat.

Our baby brother was born later that year. Mom and Dad named him Kevin. To Matt, Denny, Peggy, and me, he will always be GTO!

Amazing how our imaginations can get away from us. It is fun to daydream. Actually, it is a very good break.

Brothers Matt and Kevin with my dad, the King of Nooooo Restrictions

YOU'RE A DANNY!

My oldest son, Danny, is neither a Daniel nor a Dan. He is a Danny. As he was closing out his senior year at Mizzou, he sent me a draft of his first résumé. The first word on the page was worse than a typo. It stated his first name as Daniel.

We talked it through. Daniel's sue for numbers. Dan's count numbers. And Danny's generate numbers. In other words, Danny's were closer to dandy.

"Hello, my name is Danny" is endearing to elders as you work your way up. And it remains endearing and less intimidating to those who are your juniors as you work your way down. It is an attractive name that is authentic, personable, and appealing. And my oldest is all those things and more.

Being real is a choice. It is the only comfortable choice.

Big Iowa just shared with me the good news that Danny, his brother Jared and sister Jane are on a much better heavenly track then I was at their age.

Danny had his college selection made before kindergarten: MIZ-ZOU

Danny right after graduating from MIZ-ZOU

ONE SEMESTER MAX

My youngest son, Jared, has been a fun-loving snowboarder and paintballer for years. From when he was thirteen until he was sixteen, these pursuits involved many weekend hauls to and fro.

One day I picked up Jared and his friends, Jimmy and Parker, from the fake-snowed ski slope on the perimeter of St. Louis. The conversation drifted from snow to a challenge from Jared and Jimmy as to why Parker acted differently around his girlfriend than he did around other kids at school. When Parker volunteered he had dated this girl for six months, I chimed in with, "Fourteen-year-olds should only be allowed to date one semester, maximum."

I did not give this piece of wisdom another thought until I saw Parker two weeks later and he blurted out, "Hey, Mister O. I did what you told me and broke up with my girlfriend."

O'Brother, what did I do here?

Then to make matters even worse, Jared said, "Yeah, Dad, all the kids at school are talking about your one-semester-max rule. There's been an epidemic of breakups this week, and all the girls are mad at me." To add insult to injury, Jared reminded me that Valentine's Day was tomorrow.

We laugh about it now. It goes to show that even when you don't think teenagers are listening, they do open their ears more than we suspect. Though I never want to bring embarrassment to one of my children, I do believe in one-semester-max dating for high schoolers. However, I should limit advice to my own kids.

Jared with his sister Jane

Jared after a full day of snowboarding

JJ

As I pulled into the driveway for my first date with JJ, my first thought was: *Her parents must do quite well to afford such an impressive home in an upscale neighborhood.* After several minutes of chitchat, I asked JJ if her parents were home. She appeared a bit puzzled by the question and answered, "Yes. They are hosting a pool party." We were in her living room. I could clearly see the pool, and nobody was there. Could this house, fit for a CEO, be JJ's home? Yes! Guess what else? JJ was a CEO.

JJ was an accomplished businesswoman by the ripe age of 32, having put into play many valuable lessons learned while attending Washington University's MBA program. She also has an expressive smile and vibrant charm that she can turn on and off in a flash. Though her mane was usually rolled up, it could stretch below her waist. And she had more ambition than hair.

JJ felt sleep was for the lazy. Sleeping together, though, was gratefully acceptable. What a fascinating all-out assault on accomplishment JJ was. Energy and then some. JJ and I married within a year. We drained our frequent-flyer miles and headed to Egypt for a Nile River cruise. I was exposed to many of JJ's nice things when we returned, including a Porsche that I didn't drive because I did not know how to drive with a stick shift. I developed a special kinship with her horse, Fooler. I spent many a cig break horsing around with Fooler in the back forty.

Among my favorite things about JJ were her parents, Bob and Jane. Bob is a successful industrialist of a fourth-generation steel company that extended its reach into petroleum and banking. He looked the part, with sturdy good looks, a square jaw, and eyes that could either twinkle or go stern, depending on the task or negotiation. When he elected to be gruff, his wife, Jane, would call him

Robert instead of Bob. Jane occasionally called her daughter Roberta when her own steely side showed.

Jane grew up in Los Angeles in the '40s and '50s. Jane's babysitter, when she was little, was a soon-to-be-famous Marilyn Monroe. Marilyn's first wedding took place in Jane's parents' home. We loved Jane's stories of post-World War II Los Angeles. She brought color to St. Louis. Her wardrobe, her language, and her stories were all radiant. Tall, pretty, and very LA was Jane.

Jane's cancer began to worsen as JJ and I approached our first anniversary. She fought the good fight with diligence and charm before it won out. On the very day we would have celebrated Jane's next birthday, JJ gave birth to our daughter. The choice of Jane for her name was a natural. And she has grown up to be like her grandmother in many ways. Colorful. Pretty. And as evidenced in the next story "The Best Presentation Ever," daughter Jane is an exceptional storyteller, too. And guess what? Her destiny was Los Angeles. Currently, she is in her third year at USC, pursuing a degree in the university's prestigious film school.

I have learned many lessons from former wife number two, the top three being the power of candor, the importance of risk taking, and most importantly, forgiveness. Admission to Heaven will mean permission to see Jane again. No doubt she is there. Who knows, maybe she will introduce me to Marilyn?

BEST PRESENTATION EVER

I have seen some killer presentations while working at Maritz, Heritage, and MC2. I have studied speeches given by JFK, Martin Luther King, Ronald Reagan, and Bill Clinton with great admiration. However, my daughter made my favorite presentation in the fourth grade.

As mentioned in the previous story, my daughter, Jane, is the namesake of her colorful grandmother. My daughter's colorful character was blossoming by fourth grade. Jane attended a wonderful institution called Community School. It had provided the educational foundation for many of St. Louis's wealthier families for generations. In the carpool line, I once counted twenty-seven consecutive SUVs.

Jane came to me asking for help with a class assignment. Each fourth-grader had pulled the name of a state out of a hat and was now tasked with making a five-minute presentation about their selected state. Jane had pulled Texas.

The next evening, I returned home with an oversized piece of foam board. One of the designers at work had shaped it into an exact replica of Texas. Dressing up the board was fun. We placed stickers of Dallas Cowboys football helmets and cheerleaders in north Texas. We found a picture of the Alamo and placed it near San Antonio. Space artwork was positioned near Houston. We left eastern Texas blank but flooded west Texas with dozens of stickers of oil derricks.

Our core work completed, it was time to make this presentation memorable. First, we decided it would be more personal if Jane were to make her presentation in a Texas accent. Every private conversation we had for two weeks was an attempt to refine a distinct Texas accent. Her mimicry improved every day. Then we developed the script, which included appropriate pauses and a punch line the mothers in the audience would immediately understand was targeted at them.

American States Day finally arrived. So did eighteen students presenting eighteen states, two teachers, and fourteen moms, including Jane's recently divorced (from me) mom…and me!

Jane's drawled opening startled the crowd. These kids, parents, and teachers who had known Jane since junior kindergarten were overcome by the new voice coming from their longtime friend.

She began by mispronouncing several local streets on purpose in her Texas twang. She then directed them to a highway that led to a photo of a Dallas Cowboys cheerleader and football helmet sticker in north Texas. Then she pointed to stickers of the space program in Houston and the Alamo in "San Antone." It was her closing that elevated this presentation from extremely good to best ever. Pointing to the dozens of oil derrick stickers clustered in the western part of the state, Jane twanged, "And West Texas is clearly the most important part of the great state of Texas—as well as any ole region in the country cuz that's where we get the oil to heat our fancy homes and feed our fancy SUVs. Thankee!"

She aced it. Even then, Jane realized attention is the gateway to the brain. She brought Texas to her class in a personal and vivid way.

Like her mom, she is willing to take risks. Like her grandma, she has the charm to make things sparkle. Proud.

Jane making her "Best Ever Presentation"

Jane dresses up mighty nice

THAT TURKEY'S DONE

I prefer driving golf carts to cars. You need an engineering degree to understand all of the buttons on some of the cars I've had. In the mid-1980s, my company car was a squared-off navy blue box that my friend, Lincoln, called Blue Anger. It had a dashboard like a 747 and more buttons than I could master. The knob for the heater/air conditioner particularly troubled me.

I had several dates with a touring lounge singer playing at the local Hilton. She was a country-western singin' Kentuckian. When she spoke, I couldn't understand a word. I could, however, understand her when she sang. In conversations, I just kept my eyes on her while shaking my head with my little Asian girl smile, as if I agreed with everything.

One late spring evening with the temperatures rising, I picked up Miss Kentucky at her place. As I pulled Blue Anger away from her parking lot, she began frantically waving her arms and hooting something incoherent over and over again. I was puzzled. Finally, she sang it: "That turkey's done!" Evidently, the heat cooking us in my car was more than my sweating singer-girl could stand. So my cluelessness with a Chevrolet owner's manual cooled all intentions for that evening.

Later she scribbled some lyrics for a new song that went something like, "The only thing hot about Tee-um is his front seat..." This turkey's done. Soon we were, too.

We are blessed to live in a country with so much diversity and so many interesting regions. I applaud the adventurous who explore all of our unique places. Many gems.

A WHITE BALL, GREEN GRASS, & BLUE LIP WEDGES

I first became acquainted with the game of golf as a sixth-grader when I joined the ranks of caddies at Westborough Country Club. By the seventh grade, I was carrying two bags. By the eighth grade, I was bicycling to members' homes for poker games.

I worked fairly hard at improving my golf skills. I still keep score, but now when I reflect hole by hole on my game, my memories are more about the best line I heard or said on a given hole versus the best shot. Last week, for example, a new member asked me if I was hitting it longer because of technology. I answered, "Longer? No. but wider, yes! I used to hit it five yards in the rough. Now I am hitting it fifteen."

It has been said the quickest way to truly get to know someone is on a golf course. It is not just the quickest; it can be the best!

MIDDLE OF THE
NIGHT GOLF TIP

Eddie is one of my cost-conscious friends. That is one reason he could afford to join the Sand Hills Golf Club when it opened sixteen years ago. Eddie has hosted me at Sand Hills the past fifteen July 4th weekends. It is always two foursomes. We call ourselves the Fated Eight.

Sand Hills is unlike any other golf environment. Located in northwest Nebraska, the staff is everything Cornhusker Nation boasts: friendly, warm, and considerate. This gem was created by Dick Youngscap, and designed by Gentle Ben Crenshaw and Bill Coore.

Sand Hills is ranked the best golf course in the world built since 1960. I regard it not just as my favorite golf course, but as my favorite place in the world. Yes, I have played the highly-regarded courses of Scotland and Ireland. The only criteria by which the Irish and Scottish courses are better is that they are easier to get to.

I have saved a small fortune in sleeping aids since playing Sand Hills. When I lay awake in the middle of the night fretting about the events of the prior or following day, I happily accept the clock and play Sand Hills in my mind. I usually don't finish the front nine. Last night I teed off at 3:11 a.m. and nodded off laying five from the fringe on the brutish fourth hole.

Pick someone or someplace special to visit for nights when sleep is a toss. Then appreciate the time off. I am lucky I found my form of meditation by playing a beloved course.

COUPLES GOLF:
A HIGHER-ORDER SOLUTION?

The prior story painted a dreamy place called Sand Hills and fifteen consecutive July 4th weekends. Those getaways begin with an itinerary that is a mad twelve-hour dash with fast-driving Raybo Laidet-bo or the equally laborious air-ground hybrid of flying to Omaha and heading west in a rental car for six hours. They are followed by four days that look very much like this:

- Advil
- Golf
- Porch Burger
- Golf
- Vodka
- Golf
- Red meat, red wine
- Sleep

We do this trip for five days and talk about it for 360. I appreciate my friends' wives. Once I asked our host, Eddie, if he would entertain the possibility of inviting the ladies to join us in the rugged lands of Sand Hills. Eddie asked me to craft an itinerary. Check it out. It is a bit different than the male version. No longer the Fated Eight. When it does come to pass, it will be the Sweet Sixteen.

Day One: Kansas City, Kansas City, Here We Come

9:00 a.m.	Wagon train–like group of four SUVs departs St. Louis with outlet mall stop in Warrenton and potty stops in St. Charles, Wentzville, Foristell, Kingdom City, Booneville, and Independence.
5:00 p.m.	Arrive in Kansas City. Only eight hours to cover 230 miles!
5:00–7:30 p.m.	Freshen up.
7:30–10:00 p.m.	Shopping extravaganza at The Plaza.

Day Two: Not Driving Eighty on Route #80

8:00 a.m.	Breakfast with lecture by Leadfoot Laidet on best driving practices, including foot isometrics while flooring it, making the shoulder your friend, and avoiding cops and stops but not the schnapps.
6:00 p.m.	Arrive at Sand Hills.
6:00–8:00 p.m.	Freshen up.
8:00 p.m.	Welcome-night mixer with fashion show of all prior day purchases at Warrenton Outlet Mall and Kansas City Plaza

Day Three: Let's Play Nine!

9:00 a.m.	Breakfast.
9:30–11:30 a.m.	Freshen up.
Noon	Yoga by the Dismal River.
1:30 p.m.	Front nine scramble.
5:00–7:00 p.m.	Freshen up.
7:30 p.m.	Salad and Blush Wine Jamboree. Western attire.

Day Four: A Long Look at the Backside

9:00 a.m.	Breakfast.
9:30 a.m.–1:30 p.m.	Nine-hole alternate shot on back nine with photos taken of each couple on each tee and green
1:30–4:30 p.m.	Digital camera pass, featuring photo-ops taken on the morning nine
5:00–7:00 p.m.	Freshen up.
7:30 p.m.	Vegetarian chili cook-off with wine spritzers

Day Five: Nuthin' Dullen or Sullen in Nearby Mullen

Full day of antiquing in Mullen. Optional excursion to new K-Mart sixty-five miles away in North Platte for the adventurous. In-room dining for all to brace for following *Big Day*.

Day Six: The BIG Day

8:30 a.m.	Really early breakfast.
9:00–10:00 a.m.	Only one hour to freshen up because it is the *Big Day*.
10:30 a.m.–4:30 p.m.	Golf: all eighteen holes. And playing your own ball!
5:00-8:00 p.m.	Recovery and freshen up.
8:00 p.m.	Awards ceremony with special recognition to Best Shopper, Least Tardy, Fewest Potty Breaks, and other deserving honors.

Day Seven: Finally

Return to STL at own leisure

Okay, let's state the obvious: women and men are different. That's why the message of Doc's speech in the earlier story is so crucial in making one's most important lifetime choice. The two of you can and will be different, but hopefully not as radical as the differences in these two itineraries.

Hey, Heaven is filled with ladies and gentlemen. Gotta believe Heaven has more compatible couples than its alternative destinations.

TOMMIE & MARSHALL

I am fortunate to have joined a prestigious country club back when it was affordable. Several PGA Tour events and five assessments later, it remains my one luxury. Bellerive Country Club is a special place.

Last August, I was asked to host an important client for golf and a few drinks. The client, a well-traveled insurance executive, was having a particularly good day on the course. As he was marveling about the setting from the seventeenth tee, he asked what I liked most about Bellerive. I told him, "I really like the course, the food, and the scores and scores of great people. But, you will experience soon enough the two best things about Bellerive."

We completed our round, and I introduced the client to Tommie, Bellerive's locker room manager for the past thirty-five years. Tommie excels at making people feel good about themselves. Though fighting kidney issues and dialysis, Tommie is all about you, your kids, your round, and so on. Upon meeting Tommie, it becomes quickly evident that he cares about much more than your shoes.

We proceeded to The Grill where I introduced the client to Marshall, the strongest pourer of spirits ever. The tonic in his vodka tonics takes up less room than the lime. You wouldn't want to be the Schweppes salesperson calling on the Bellerive account. County Cab makes a fortune picking up members who have ordered just two of his drinks.

The client was an astute observer. He quickly had experienced two favorite things about Bellerive. His wink about elder gentlemen Tommie and Marshall said it all. He gets it. So do they!

Special places can be very good. Special faces make them shine even better.

Flanked by two of Bellerive's finest: Tommie & Marshall

THE HILLS OF BEVERLY

We always have a celebration when we land a new account. We haven't stopped celebrating the outstanding people at Hilton Hotels since landing their Hilton Honors business five years ago. Hilton people are the best.

One of the outstanding things about Hilton is their commitment to community. One of their benefactors is City of Hope. The platform is a celebrity golf tournament, which includes two nights at the Beverly Hills Hilton, two days at Riviera Country Club, and a celebrity hosts each foursome. Wow!

A famous hotel. A famous golf course. And our celebrity is a not-so-famous actor. Now, I really enjoy staying and playing at the Beverly Hills Hilton and Riviera, but my very favorite item of the week is not a place, but a person. It's our celebrity, Richie. He's been the host for the Maritz foursome every year.

An actor. A character actor. And a real character. Richie is all three. And he is fun. I have given some thought to moving to LA. If I do, I will find someplace small near Richie in Beverly Hills. I have a feeling it would include some weekend screaming at TVs about mind-altering bad beats in the NFL.

The very nicest places become even better when they include wonderful people like the folks from Hilton and Richie. One of the reasons I've asked Big Iowa to give it his best shot is I hear this heaven place sounds pretty good. I have it visualized as just a notch below Riviera and the Beverly Hilton.

A day in paradise with Hilton's CK, Maritz' Lori,
movie star Richie and Maritz pal Victor.

SHEEP DIP

An elegant Tennessee gentleman named Junior MacDougall has hosted a prestigious golf tournament for decades. It takes place every other year in northern Michigan at the tranquil Belvedere Club. He calls the event the Sheep Dip. Though most of the foursomes are stacked with the nobility of the mid-South, he does allow St. Louisan Ricky Meyer and two additional Midwestern teams. In 2003, Ricky asked Red Heat, Doc Rames, and me to round out his team. It is not an invitation one declines.

The welcome evening event is as southern as northern Michigan can get. Discussions center around SEC football, business, and upcoming autumn cotillions. Tension builds as all await the moment Junior reveals the big board listing the matches to be played the following two days. He announces separate cash payouts for the winning team each day along with the following evening's "swish" tournament. We would soon discover the last item was to be a card game with a distinct Tennessee home-field advantage.

Throughout supper, I sat next to Junior's brother, Wiley. Wiley MacDougall is a gentleman. And Wiley was more than just his name. It was a description. When Junior undraped the big board, I discovered my opponent the following day would be Roy Moore Jr.

When I asked Wiley if he knew Roy, Wiley rose from the table and scanned the crowd. He finally pointed to an elderly gentleman who looked like his best days were behind him. Then Wiley very slowly placed his hands across his heart and said slowly, "Of awl the fine gentleman in this room, and of awl the fine gentleman I have ever encountered, never have I met a finer gentleman nor a finer golfer than Roooy Moooore Junior. He has won the State of Tennessee championship four times, the Tennessee Mid-Amateur five times, and has been a fixture at the United States Amateur more times than I can count. Now, you seem like a fine lad, Timma, but you will have more than your hands full tomorrow."

The next morning I introduced myself to the legend on the driving range. I told Roy that Wiley had laid out an incredible pedigree of his accomplishments. Then I shared my own record of limited success: unimpressive small field victories in the 1992 Spanky and a 1996 Mixed Member. He replied like a gentleman: "Had not heard of the Spanky, but I am sure it was something special." He had never played in a Mixed Member, so I clearly had an edge there. Though the match was a destined loser the night before, it took a turn for the worse when I had a gimme for birdie on the first five-par, only to see Roy swish his wedge from 110 yards for eagle.

Unfortunately, my spanking did not stop at the course. At nightfall, we were introduced to a Southern card game called Swish. It is a combination of Hold 'em, In Between, and Guts. My dad had always warned me, "Timmy, yes, you are good at cards. Maybe you are even very good. And very good at cards is just good enough to lose a very lot."

Well, the drinks were free, and so were the Heat, Doc, and I—as in free of any money in our wallets after losing every red cent! We drank quite a bit, and it helped us justify our losses. Because there were three teams from St. Louis, some of the gentleman distinguished our four-man St. Louis team the St. Louis Dronks. I think they meant it affectionately because it sounded much nicer with their sweet southern pronunciation. Also, *Dronks* was a pretty major statement as one of the other St. Louis teams was captained by a gentleman who just the prior week had the following unfortunate exchange on the side of a highway with an officer of the law. It went something like this: "Do you know how fast you're going, sir?" His drawled reply said something like seventy. Then, the officer weighed in with "No, you were maxing out at fifteen". So, we had stiff competition to be tagged as the *Dronks*!

All of us retired that evening penniless from that *swishy* Tennessee card game. Red Heat was the first to awaken the next morning. I woke up to him going through the pockets of the pants I had worn the prior evening. Then I foggily watched him raid my golf bag. He knew I usually used dimes as ball marks. He looked like he had hit the jackpot when he discovered twelve dimes that he could use to buy a newspaper and small coffee.

It was the final day. Gratefully, our entry fees had been paid the first evening. Against all odds, our foursome combined for birdie after birdie and posted a round that easily won the final day's event. Always a spiller and a thriller, Red Heat was particularly hot that day. He spilled 'em in from all parts. Doc drilled 'em in, too. And Rickey willed 'em in.

I was the first in our foursome to hit the lunchroom. A sweet southern hush was going through the crowd with soft smiles and positive head nods repeating, "You don't say. The Dronks won. The St. Louis Dronks. Well, that's just fine and dandy cuz their pockets needed fillin'. Maybe they'll try their luck with some Swish again tonight."

Tennessee is home to some of the classiest people I have ever met. This group that graces the classy climes of northern Michigan is world class. They were very gracious about our comeback. Golf tournaments, like life, are about taking advantage of good breaks and overcoming the bad ones. And best to partner in both with a team that can spill, drill, and will their way to a win!

THE KALMER ONE

Though a long-time observer of lust at first sight, I did not believe in love at first sight until August 24, 2001. It arrived in the form of the Kalmer One at a popular watering hole called Schneithorst's, St. Louis' version of the Hofbrau House. Freshly divorced, this smiling, stylish mother of four talented young men lit up the room and those surrounding her. I had rarely pressed discoveries like this. Columbus must have felt a similar sensation as he approached our shores.

Having the nerve to make contact with the Kalmer One proved life changing. I had never met a woman so attractive who could also bring funny, caring, and good cheer to the table. I call her the Kalmer One for three reasons: first, Kalmer is her maiden name; second, she never embraced my original nickname for her: the White Oprah; and third, she is calmer than I, and the trillion folks who are calmer than I am but not as calm as she!

About an hour into our first visit, the Kalmer One smiled and exclaimed, "We have so much in common. You are Irish Catholic, and I am German Catholic." She was funniest at times like this when it was unintentional. She seemed puzzled by my response: "Do you know how Mercedes Benz automobiles would be different if they were built in Ireland instead of Germany? Their engines would hurl and not hum, but they would have better cup holders and bigger ashtrays." She would come to experience the stereotypical differences between these two ethnicities soon enough.

In our sixth year together, we made our first visit to Los Angeles. I told her I couldn't wait until we walked Rodeo Drive and watched heads turn wondering who she used to be. I meant it as a compliment. She took it as a dig. Picture a younger version of Lucy, Goldie, or Farrah. Or a slightly older Jennifer or Chelsea. Or all of them rolled into one. We visited Los Angeles twice, and I saw many double takes. I was right.

I have several 9/11-related associations with the Kalmer One. Our first official date was originally scheduled for September 11, 2001. It was a horrific day for America and the entire planet. Overcome by the day's events, we rescheduled for four days later. Our romantic comedy ran for nine years and eleven months. It was smoked by my twin towers of booze and cigs. The Kalmer One replaced Operation Needs Tim with Operation Needs Time. Amazing what a difference one little vowel can make.

O'Well. We forge ahead with glee because the two of us have a lot of it. And both of us are fortunate to have DNA that welcomes glad and filters sad. So we will bounce, not trounce or pounce!

THE PRESENT IS A PRESENT

Some people live for the past. Some moan for the future. The happiest people I know are all about the present. One of my favorite actors is Owen Wilson. I first loved him in *Shanghai Noon* when he scolded his bungling gang with, "A good plan today is better than a great plan tomorrow."

We all have lessons that teach us to live each day. One such lesson came to me in the form of a car accident that killed a best friend when he was a rookie playing for the Steelers. Randy had been regarded as the toughest guy in the state. As a result, there were continual challengers. He never started a fight, but I did watch him finish more than a few, usually quickly. To say he was durable was an understatement. If a car wreck could overpower him, anything could happen to anyone.

Randy became the first of my inner circle who I lost to either Heaven or Purgatory thirty-five years ago. His jersey indicated he was number 91. As a person, he had an even bigger percentile. He wouldn't need someone as persuasive as Big Iowa to take on St. Peter.

Live each day not as if it is your last, but your favorite. Even Mondays. TGIMM: a.k.a. Thank God it's Monday morning!

HEAVY DOORS & HEAVY POURS

The most famous street between our coasts is Michigan Avenue. World-class shops, museums, hotels, and parks flank it. When I was asked to open an office for Heritage in Chicago, I chose a Michigan Avenue address to validate our legitimacy.

The office was a short walk from a favorite hotel. The Chicago Hilton became home four nights a week for six months. Everything about this palace was strong, including its doors and its pours.

First, the doors. You have probably stayed at hotels with room doors offering the protection of a curtain. Not the Chicago Hilton. They are baroque and sound like they belong on a Cadillac when they shut.

Maybe it is because I am a Virgo, but one of my quirks is to rid my hotel room of room service trays immediately after consuming the food. On one memorable morning, room service arrived just as I was getting out of the shower. Clad in nothing more than drips that had yet to be toweled, I quickly ate and began to place the tray in the hall. Suddenly, the room door rear-ended me into a hallway somersault. Perhaps a heavier rump could have withstood this attack.

I was as naked as I was nervous in a hotel hallway. What to do? The napkin with egg yolk quickly became my frontal friend. A back cover of USA Today became my own back cover. The one hundred steps to a hall phone were long, yet blessedly quiet. A bellman with a master key soon arrived and averted disaster. He sheepishly claimed, "Not to worry, sir. Happens all the time." Empathetic bellman. Pathetic guest.

So strong doors can be a feature rather than a benefit. Same with strong pours. The Hilton is home to my favorite hotel bar in the country, Kitty O'Shea's.

Most of the staff is on loan from Ireland and packing Green Cards. The place is loaded with cheer. Irish music rules each night except for a break called open mic. Guest participation is encouraged. Sporting attempts to sing, jig, tap, or story are enthusiastically received.

After several weeks, I was considered a regular and began to participate in open mic. My monologue included revised lyrics to tunes from *The Sound of Music*. The bartender described my accompanying moves as half jig and half tap. Others called them awkward. Still others called them unusually awkward. The songs were a United Nations collision: too many scotches meeting Austrian ballads in an Irish bar. My remake of "I am Sixteen going on Seventeen" is disturbing to this day.

Gratefully, my day job was going very well. The staff in our Chicago office quickly flourished, requiring more space and a move to the suburbs. Seven months passed without a visit to Kitty O'Shea's. Then one day I retrieved my mail and opened the loveliest Christmas card. It featured a large photograph of the Kitty O'Shea's staff and their signatures. And in big, bright green ink it stated, "Hey Timmy, We Haven't Seen You in Seven Months. Assume You Are Dead."

Two obvious lessons from Chicago: first, returning room service trays is a fully clothed sport, and even then, don't let the door hit you on the way out; and second, don't let geography stall strong connections. Make today's technology your friend to enable closeness, even when the smiles and miles are counties or countries apart.

NEXT

In preparing this book, I have shared these stories with many friends and family members. Each has weighed in with mention of other real experiences of mine that they believe have more entertainment value. I remind them that the premise of *Tobacco Is Not a Vegetable* is to make the case for earning selection into Heaven versus the more likely detour through Purgatory. As such, I omitted some of the "line-crossing" stories. Also, I have omitted some incredibly special people from work, home, and play. So that sets up a sequel. For now, we can call it *Tobacco Is Not a Vegetable II*. It might be rated R. Who knows? It may address Purgatory versus Hell instead of Heaven. Much more to follow...

THE ANNEX?
GOOD ENOUGH FOR ME

Is this actually happening? Is this real or surreal? *Tim O'Neill v. Purgatory* is in session and nearing its conclusion. I admire the calming Big Iowa as he strolls with confidence from the podium to his chair. He has faced off with a battle-tested veteran from St. Peter's team. She wears a nametag stating "St. Dolores, Vice President of Admissions." Yes, she brought forth a bevy of witnesses hell-bent on a destination choice different than mine. Big Iowa somehow cracked their credibility. It was amazing, as from what I could recall they should have been spot on. The difference maker in the trial was the impressive life lessons learned from the precious folks featured in *Tobacco is not a Vegetable*.

The characters of *Tobacco is not a Vegetable* are winners. And now, so am I ... well, sort of. After being asked to rise, St. Dolores also stood and barked, "We are not quite ready for you to use the Pearl Entrance, but we are granting you access to one of the plots we recently acquired from Purgatory. It is officially Heaven, but sort of an annex. Some of your new neighbors who were recently promoted from the Purg call it 'Heaven's Hybrid.'" Then she directed me to "make that path over there—the one just like your life, with three long lefts and a quick right at the very end."

As I took to the path, I overheard St. Dolores' assistant St. Marta mutter to St. Peter, "That rule Baby Jesus came up with two thousand years ago about confessions and forgiveness is filling this place up with too many Catholics."

Amen.

I was a plaidie. Brother Matt always looked stylish in stripes. Credit Matt and his talented team at Phoenix Creative for designing the book cover.

17956571R00066

Made in the USA
Lexington, KY
07 October 2012